CIRCUMFERENCE

CIRCUMFERENCE

Keith Howden

PENNILESS PRESS PUBLICATIONS

Published by
Penniless Press Publications 2020

© Keith Howden

The author asserts his moral right to be identified as the author of the work. All rights reserved. No part of this publication may be reproduced, stored in a retrieval system or transmitted in any form or by any means, electronic, mechanical, photocopying, recording or otherwise, without the prior permission of the publishers.

ISBN 978-1-913144-23-4

Cover: by Keith Howden

For Iris

Diamond Wedding

2020

Circumference

A Lexicon for the Fisher King	9
Lo Tsen's Map of Lyonnesse	11
A double helix for Pendragon	13
The Geologies of Illusion	15
The Satnav fails Camelot	17
Forged Metaphor	19
The Range Finder	21
Within the Sun's Wheel	22
The Dalmatian Queen	24
The Queen as Whore	26
The League Table	27
Did you want a seat?	29
A History of the Merlin Engine	31
A Sorcerer's Fabrication	32
1.The Lancelot Equilibrium	33
2. A Grammar for Love	35
3. A Grammar for Lust	36
Elaine makes it to Page Three	38
1. The Percival Paradigm	39
2. Nearly a Happening	41
1. The Galahad Entropy	42
2. And did it ever matter?	44
A Million and One Maps	46
Not bloody Gawain	50

A New Cartography of Logres	52
Do you fancy a drink?	53
A Cup's Circumference	54
Morgan le Fay: My Sonar Acrobatics	56
Morgana: The Echo of an Echo	58
Morgause: A Guide to Royal Incest	59
A Handbook for Mycologists	61
What you wear is what you are	63
A Diploid Algebra	65
Mere Manipulation	67
Nimue sees Darwin right	69
Making a Splash	70
An Allegorical Analogue	72
The Thigh in the Wound	74

A Lexicon for the Fisher King

'Somewhere,' the wrecked King said, 'exists
a language of transcendence, a dialect
to unwreck me. Somewhere, an enigma speech
that is itself a healing will reverse
this dolorous stroke. Somewhere,' he said,
are transactions beyond the sayable
where words cannot gain, that cannot happen
within the tightened knots of grammar.
'Somewhere,' the wrecked King said, 'exists
circumference, a grail tongue that rides beyond
mere consciousness, beyond the waste
of Listeneuse. I seek that language.

In it, the bent light secreting Carbonek
will be straightened, the one true quester
will consume his prize. In this hallelujah
lives my hope's genesis. The wrecked King
is unwrecked, the small streams of his veins
irrigate the land, the great arteries
pumping within him become broad rivers
bubbling with salmon, the waste flesh of his realm
again sings fertility. I await,' he said,
'my unwrecking, the metaphor of my release.'

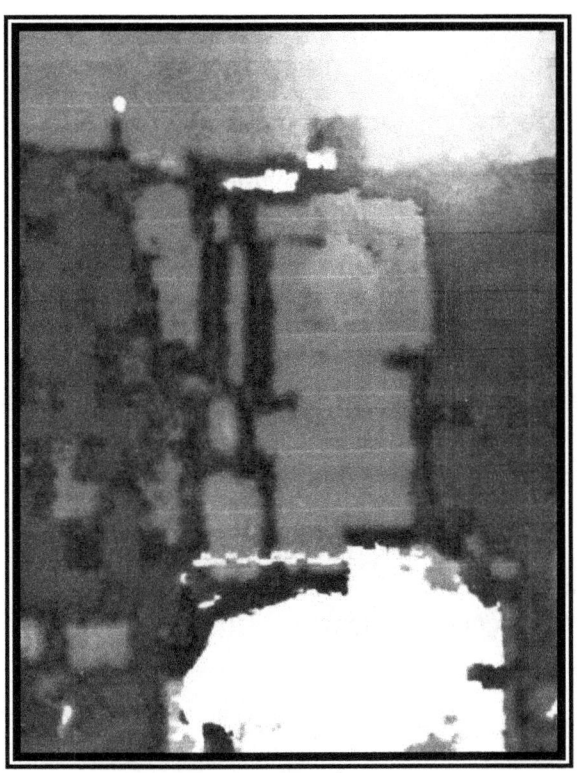

Lo Tsen's Map of Lyonesse

'There have been,' (*the girl said*), 'many maps
where maps tell only their makers' minds.
Some called it *Tir na nOg*. They mapped
no country for old men. Salmon bubbled
rich rivers, there were golden birds. The young
copulated freely. It was common knowledge
that all the certainties of age and illness
lived outside their map.
                      Others charted it,'
(*the woman said),* 'as Lubberland, or some,
Cockaigne. They mapped a pleasure ground
of cakes and ale. Licence and disorder

were their good government. Nobody left.
All were too idle or too gross or drunk
to seek escape.
                Its more serious maps,'
(the old woman said), 'were shared by those
who dreamed it *Lyonesse*. Their mapping
displayed the proper balances of equality
to shape behaviour. They knew that
to leave their map was to invite
the world's corruption.
                        For us,' *(Lo Tsen said)*,
'we mapped it *Shangri La*. It was
our refuge of culture. Our arts flourished,
our science and philosophy prospered.
Peace and tranquility were the dominants
of our map-making. You see in my rot
the inevitable consequence of leaving...'

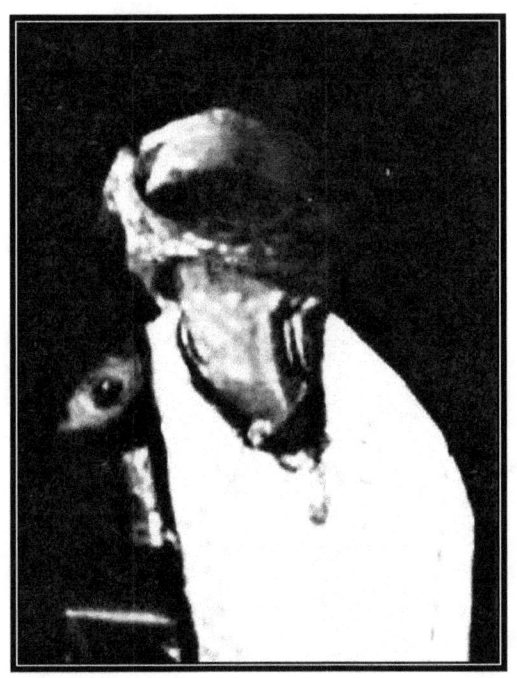

A Double Helix

'This first,' he said, 'is matters of war,
affairs of state. Sortilege foretold it:
a star of magnitude, a globe of fire
blazing a dragon's frame. From its left eye,
a ray encompassing Gaul to my command.
From its right eye, a beam of molten light
asserting my possession of the Welsh
and Irish lands. Under these omens,
I danced the Dragon my device to serve
my purposes in future war.
                              This second,
is matters of war, affairs of state.
No star of magnitude saw it: no dragon frame
came near. A candle led me to her room.

I wore her husband's shape a black art
stole me from Hell. Within her bed,
I entered her and spat into her womb
a future king, a son to dance my Dragon
and serve my purposes in future war.'

The Geologies of Illusion

Ersatz in fables' frost,
arctic in story ice,
rock pinnacles affect a citadel.
Chance stone assembles walls
that melt to bare a camp's rammel
of wood and clay. A never King
musters unarmoured knights
in nowhere's petty kingdom,
to chasten and subdue
a clan's barbarous intrigues.

Or in romance's lies of errantry
welds an interior journey,
frames a dream dynasty to contrive
swords still sanguine to roods
and disciplines of chivalric honour,
where ghost rallying of warlords
and mercenary metals ride uneasy,
congealed in henge landscapes,
gelid in warlock woods.

The Satnav fails Camelot

'I am,' the mound said,' *mud*. My music
is infinitely fluid. No geography
refines me: no archaeologies fix
my state's dimensions. My co-ordinates
dice in fabulous games. Hear my declensions:
conjugate my devices. I am bizarre.
I am *mud*. I ferment a lost order's harmony
and palisade inquiry. My invisible gates

lead only to the unfindable. I am
foul and celestial, a myth's paradox,
illusion's rainbow utopia.
I am the mind's firmament haunting
ineffable galaxies. I am *mud*.'

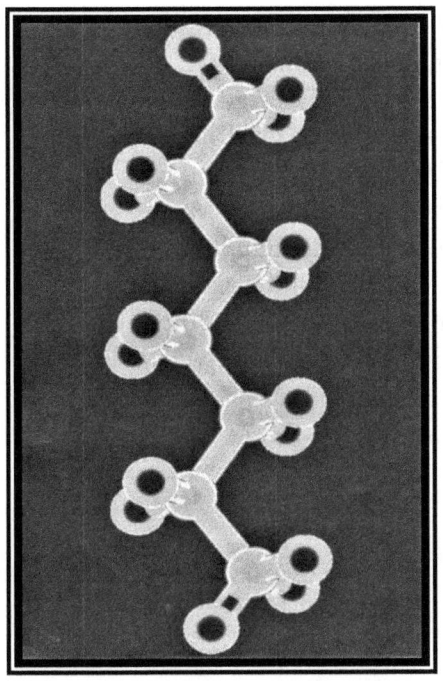

Forged Metaphor

'I am,' the blade said, 'the seven braided.
I am made as poems are forged
in the arcane alchemies of metaphor.
I am the mind's metal spun transcendent
and elastic within the helix structures
of my being. I am fused circumference.
I am shaped lexicon and logos
of the ores' gift, am seven formulas
of conjuration's speech. The Seven Sisters
of the Arch were midwives at my birth.
Earth word and *air word*, *fire word* and *water word*
consecrated my forging. The sun's chemistries
and the moon's mysteries, the stars' ache

and the spheres' symmetries are welded
within me. At my solstice making,
each swore and blessed. The first spoke *Harmony,*
the second, *Reason* and the third *Benevolence.*
One promised *Destiny.* Another
hailed me *Celestial.* Then came *Amen*
and *Omen.* Which among them knew
my esemplastic anneal? Who was it shaped
epiphany within the cauldron's seethe? I am
seven banded. Seven smiths spelled my sleight.'

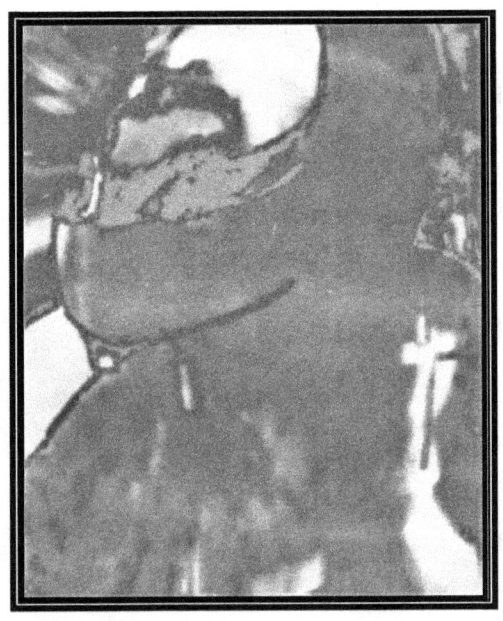

The Range Finder

'In the combustions of the present,' he said,
'how do I turn? The old dispensation's charts
lead to a waste land. *Where are the maps?*
I would rule well. Do I then succour
froth galaxies of diviners proposing
arcane solutions from their fairy utopias?
Or those vinegar ascetics urging
a joyless heaven? Do I sleep within
a pentagram or embrace a cross?
Is there no algebra to grease dilemma,
some almanac that might pilot my ignorance
through our ailment's turbulence? I have learned
that the celestial and imperial city
has no sound foundation. We dither now
on a frontier of choice. *There are no maps.'*

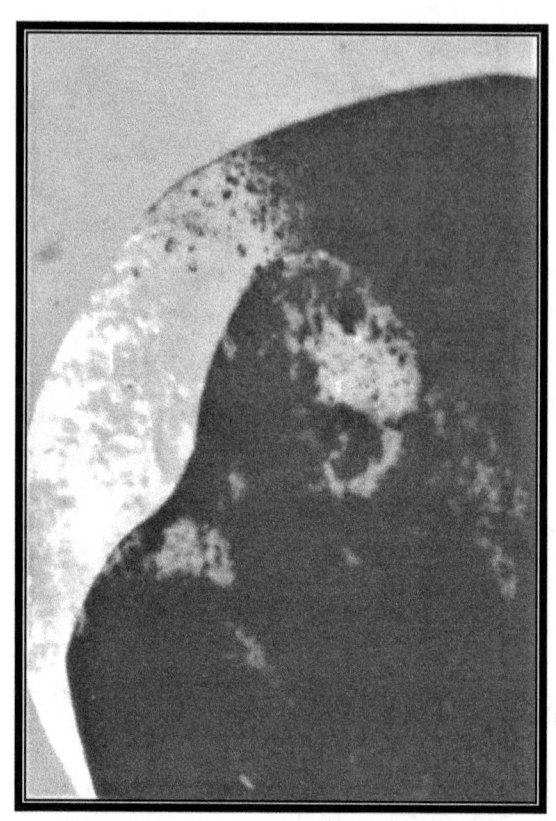

Within the sun's wheel.

He inhabits now a blown
sun's wheel, broods on
his dynasty's disaster and
the mess of things. He knows
his queen a whore, his table
shrivelled to barrel-top,
the Grail's lost litanies now
no more than a myth's toy

in a whirling world. The old
insurgencies rear a wasp's nest
of rivalries. He dreams
sorcery's new struggle, a blade's
scythe in sunlight to quell
an adder's hiss where magic
augurs Mordred's thrust,
Excalibur thrown to a wet den
and a ferry already decked
to tote a corpse's metaphor
through uncertain channels
to Avalon's other geographies.'

The Dalmatian Queen

She dresses black and white.
The romance assembling her
demands dramatic duality
to port the rise of kingdoms
and the lure of beds, someone
to carry the can for the rot
of heroic dreams, to provide
myth's landing strip for pilot error.
Day gauzes her in sunlight,
parading Camelot's mud

as restraint's figurehead, always
at ceremony's right hand.
Night clothes her nakedness in
a vampire anarchy dribbling
order's juice on bedsheets.
She arches the lie and truth
of matters and treads
a tragicomic tightrope wearing
under her skirts, between
her thighs, the necessary breach
of Arthur's fief illusion.

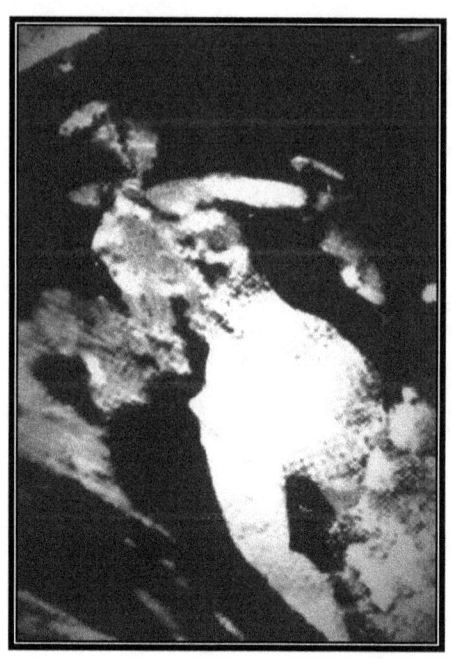

The Queen as Whore

'My love,' she said, 'how would your pleasure be?
Which way do you most desire me? Does a Queen's
near nakedness erect you? Does my regal flesh
flare your lust? See now what my fronds
have earlier concealed from you, touch what
my silks have hidden. I desire you. Fondle me.
Set yourself now between my opened thighs
to have what you want of me. I shall move
royally to your thrust. Let a Queen's quim
moist and imperial swell unarmoured
to take your sword. Oh my love,' she said,
I have long desired you. Take me now.'

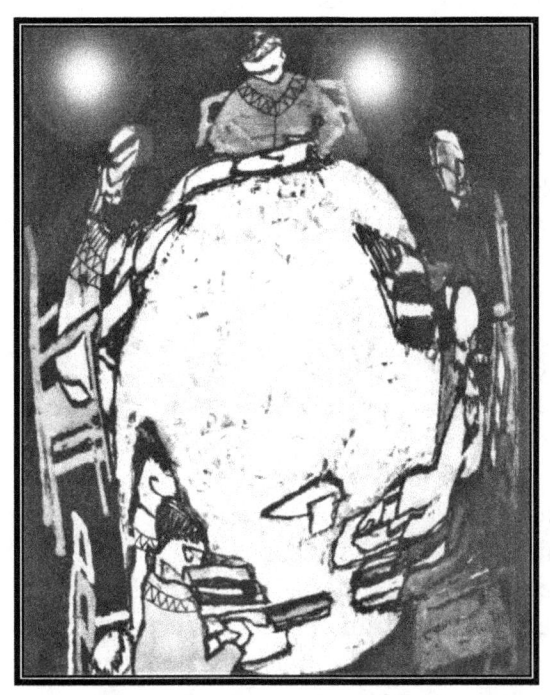

The League Table

'Learn me,' the table said, 'I am the earth's spin.
Organic in my marquetries are fixed
all myths, all maps, all histories. My making
crams every geography. All species
cavort my forests, every projection
of every celestial city finds its alleys
within my oak. *Learn me.* See here
where shabby carpentries provoke Leviathan
levering: here squats Troy : there Helen weeps
a thousand ships and Achilles sulks.
Black astronomies are clattering
the vault. See here, in creaking joints,
unicorns bawl and Babylon blisters

suspended gardens: Nebuchadnezzar
reeks in his tomb: the suave Euphrates
swallows sand. Comets are spluttering
their maledictive omens. See here,
in wrinkled veneers, Behemoth bellows:
Carthage droops beneath a weight of elephants:
Hannibal rots a thespian moon's
cold ceremonies. See here where scars
and old distresses corrupt: Jerusalem
slithers to faith: a cockatrice screeches:
Judas palms new parables and stars
blazon a blank Golgotha. See here,
where woodworm churns my flank. Rome rises:
glib bestial heresies and heraldries
strut marble: a Pontiff's broken promise
slays millions where the Tiber
scratches its arse on sculptured stone. Planets
whirl helix in a helix universe.
Learn me,' the table said, 'the galaxy's handmaid.
I am all charts, all projections. In me
are all co-ordinates and cosmologies. Endless space
twists in my magnetism. The zodiac
rattles in my celestial arteries.'

Did you want a seat?

'It turned up,' the curator said, 'in some
tin tabernacle in Wales. It had been
one of a set. The others were rotting round it,
punk to the touch, a long-since finished feast
for woodworm, swaying or collapsing
in a manure of their own sawdust.
Perfect in every detail and undamaged,
rock solid and unmarked, just as good
as the day it was carved. And that,' he said,
'is where our problems start. It's a wood

we've never met before. The grain's tattoo
has patterns that we can't yet understand
or calculate the nature of its growth.
It's not an English wood. Not European.
Our Indian and Asian experts tell us
it's one they've never seen. In the Museum
there's been a tale of a night-watchman
who slept in it and never woke. It's true
that if a fly or any insect touches it
it shrivels almost at once. Most of our cleaners
won't go near it. They talk of static
and electric spasms. The daft ones think
it's radio-active and one of their wits
calls it the *Siege Perilous* ...'

A History of the Merlin Engine

Magically rigged,
he builds a conjured face
to mask his features' ambiguity
and dreams a stone, a Grail,
Excalibur's enchanted blade
to shear the tangled chain that irons
the gates of elsewhere's garden.
He strides a promontory
unknown to latitude and longitude,
that pricks uncharted seas
whose rival tides
wrangle and knot to blend
his blood's equivocation

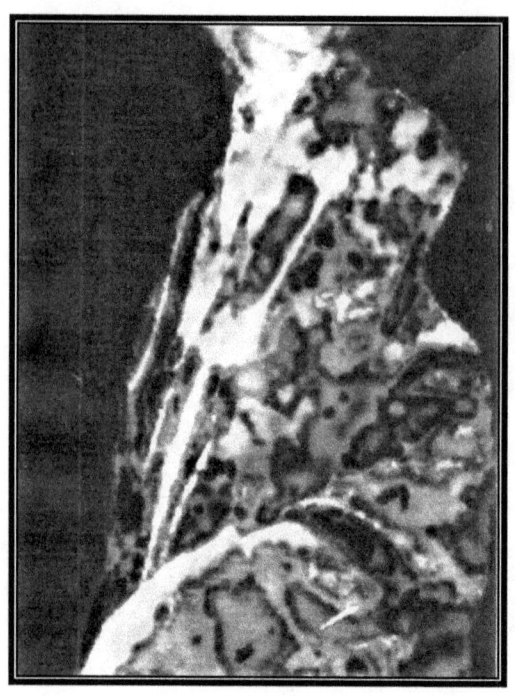

A sorcerer's fabrication

'This cloak,' he said, sings sorceries. It is
alchemy's chart and calculates the rituals
of a simpler sun, the squandered northings
and eastings of the buried stars. It clothes
a once music of the soul's million maps.
It shapes no known horizons, frames no distance
or scale: its contours veil an older code
of height and depth. No compass points
its miracle dimensions. It robes
every illusion, tells all myths and mysteries
in an arcane cipher. *Few read it safely.*'

1. The Lancelot Equilibrium

Such pilgrimages, haunted
dalmatian through a grail landscape,
document no door from boudoir
to Chapel. He jousts time,
skewbald in shifting weathers.
Arthur's hired hitman, flawed
chevalier of curtained couches,
mantles his silver dalliance
in a queen's flesh. But that
maradonna lance-hand falters,
scraping coarsely to misspell
ideal or *honour* on the idyll's page.
Old photographs validate

his blemish where always,
outside the plate's virginity,
a shadow stains the negative,
and always, even in snapshots,
the developer's processes
cannot erase the death's head
grinning pillion to his quest.

2. A Grammar for Love

'All things,' he said, 'burgeon the seeds
of their destruction. *Knighthood,'* he said:
'a cul-de-sac of barbarism for dullards.
Chivalry: a back-alley of pretensions,
a theatre for popinjays and fops.
Arthur's table: a roundabout for a failed
traffic of hedonism. Even the *Grail:*
a motorway for trophy-hunters, a chaos,
an entropic highway for the legion
of baboons that quested, a delirium
and a device outside transcendence.
Now let me mention *Love:* I have known
its deep diet. What did I learn from it?
How could I guess that love would be the agent
of disorder and rebellion, be a treachery
of its clean origin? And even now,
she obsesses me, possesses me, haunts
my armour with her love's circumference.'

3. A Grammar for Lust

Behind lowered eyes, her women
translate the minstrels' code. It was
no simpering seduction, modest
between maiden sheets. Hard-nippled,
damp in the crutch and hot
for satisfaction, Astolat's tart
undresses, aching to haul
buck Lancelot between her knees.
They know the unspoken dimensions
of tale and truth, the acreage
of chivalry's cool whispering and
the eavesdropped gasping behind

knight-errantry's curtain. She comes
shameless and panting to him.
They know the squeal necessities
of flesh, the sorceries of lust,
that courtly gestures in a tale's romance
disguise the buffet of arses,
the truth and smells of beds,
with a lie's lacquer and confection's
panoplies to costume a shag.

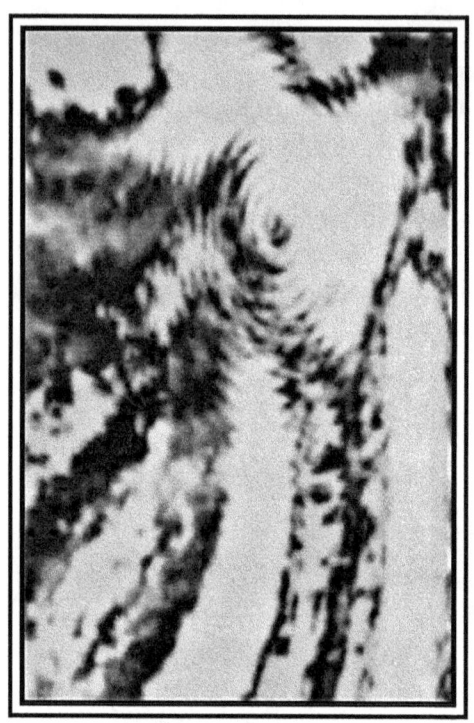

Elaine makes it to Page Three

'Those were,' she said, 'when I was young, my breasts,
upturned and firm and panting for his touch,
dreaming their fondle under his hand.
Those were,' she said, 'when I was young, my bright
and unbrowned nipples pointing their hope
of his lips' suck. Such days are long gone.
I craved his soon arrival, his nakedness
lying beside my own, his pulse within me.
That day I saw him ride the long lanes
between bright barley fields. He rode handsomely
but never came. Not long afterwards,
I married. I never loved my husband.'

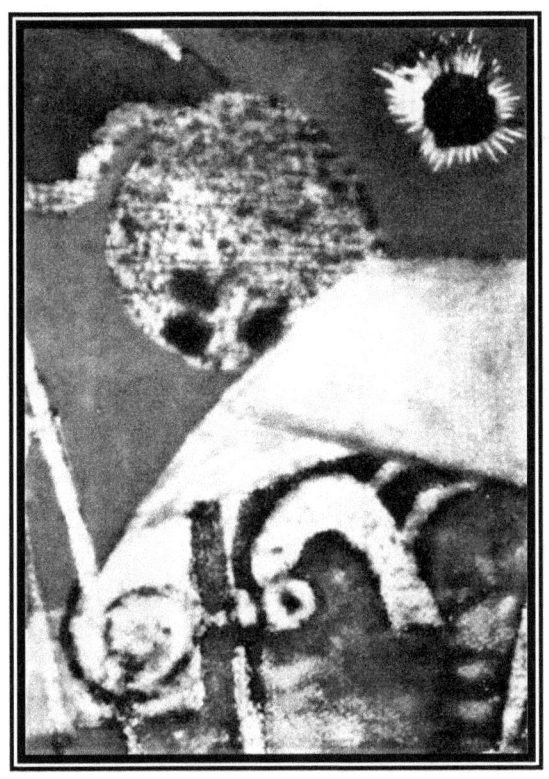

1. The Percival Paradigm

A round table's pretend
democracy begets a rustic,
a dung-foot treading equivocal
cowshit into court carpets, who
must make it nearly to the top
and by hazard win his spurs.
Errantry bibles a clod too daft
to grasp the Grail's wound,
who blunders past the cup
and then, through divine gaucherie
retrieves Calvary's spear.
Chastity's parable evolves

a virgin guilelessness to dodge
meat's snares and, green chaste,
avoid sleek seductions. Then
Chivalry fine tunes his duality.
Too vegetable to squat
The *Siege Perilous,* he passes
Romance's assault course and
naivete succeeds. Not by chance,
paradox grooms him to be
Camelot's lurch visitor to grace.

2. Nearly a Happening

'Something,' he said. 'Yes. *Something* happened.
I can't say what. No simple explanations.
Perhaps a birth and a death. I joined to fight.
I believed in Arthur's cause and quests
were not what I wanted. But something happened.
Lancelot winked. Galahad polished his soul.
A circumference, an esemplastic something,
an epiphany. Everything changed. A new
dimension exploded where the impossible
became possible. Some curvature
in time and space. Only a glow? Only
a flash of light or some misunderstood
and radiant second? Did we go all that way
to find a broken cup? And was that it?
I felt an invocation of almost....'

1. The Galahad Entropy

Heaven's harnessing strap him
tight from misdemeanour,
in unpierceable armour. He moves
visored to cross temptation's
landscapes. White-haloed,
under a white sun's aureole,
relentless in a sparer light
that eats the blood's needs,
he scales rainbows to earn
circumference with marching stars,
withholding a face that denies
the world's mirrors. The fist

that scorns the apple unsheathes
to slice the snake. He rides
unshadowed to that austere
appointment with a tin cup
in a glass country beyond
Camelot's prancing, outside
plastic honour and vows, beyond
Astolat's shabby bedrooms or
Excalibur's wet nest, even further
than Avalon's sanitary mirage.

2. And did it ever matter?

'Chastity,' he said, 'can be selective.
That's why I'm here in Sarras. Did you guess
I faked my death? *Of course I did.* I hated
flags and banners, round tables, lifted lances,
Arthur's ceremonials. His *Siege Perilous*
was uncomfortable. Did you guess
I loathed it? *Of course I did.* And then there was
the business with the Grail. Was it a cup?
Most of it, I've forgotten. Was it a bowl,
or some Welsh cauldron? And does it matter?

They all took what they wanted from it,
saw what they wanted to see. Some of them swore
they'd seen the Host. One saw a potion promising
immortality. The most hysteric claimed
it held the Magdalene's menstrual blood.
Did you guess I never cared for women?
Of course, I didn't. But here there's no shame
and no hypocrisy on that score. Our tables
aren't circular. John is my partner...'

A million and one maps

1.

'Of Sarras,' the cartographer said,
'there are as many maps as makers.
It lies flat with magnificent mountains:
it offers a sandy and accessible coast
where cliffs prohibit entry except
to the most experienced mariners. It is green:
it is a desert. It is simultaneously
barren and fertile, benign or hostile,

honest and corrupt. Its peoples are fierce.
and also gentle. They are cultured
and savage. Its parables display
an omniscient but benevolent creator:
its myths suggest a cruel and indifferent
manipulator of life. Permutate
these circumferences and you may draft
a map of Sarras. Maps dream their makers.'

2.

'We shaped,' the knight said, 'a map. But how
translate a quest into a mythic landscape?
Would we learn here some outcrop faith, or there
a river's sacrament ? Can there be charts
that encompass, in flat correlatives,
the uncopiable lattices whose grids
contrive a pilgrim labyrinth in dimensions
of the spirit, that have no northings, eastings,
the transubstantiating zones that spur
the soul's rememberings? *I mean that map.*
But by what magic logarithm can
a miracle be textured? And how read a map
so integral that subliminally it charts

the questing self, where all the past's
allegiances and sureties lie traceable
and esemplastic in its codes? *I mean a map*
whose arcane undertaking is a parable
and triple parthenogenesis whose trope
is the circumference and Grail of its own making...'

(*illustration: carving by Joe Burrows*)

Not bloody Gawain

'*Forget Gawain,*' he said, 'that pious
prosody. It was the god-lot squealing
for a piece of my altar. *No go.*
I keep my bucking feasts. My verse
parses outside their seasons' hymns.
I fire the green fuse yearly igniting
sap's deep dynamite. *Forget Gawain,*
that academic envoy. The psalm-suckers
sang to usurp my rituals, to geld
my lust inside their castrate parables.
No go. Never a fair exchange. I don't
dance monotheism and my cadences

won't fit their rhythm. I am the enigma
impelling the tree to leaf. *Forget Gawain,*
that hallelujah heresy. The anthem-boys
fancied my anarchies tamed. *No go.*
No frozen orisons, no sterile litanies.
I am the sun's missionary. I blaze
barley's ferment, the zeppelin swell
ballooning the seed, the underground
appetite of roots. *Forget Gawain.*'

A New Cartography of Logres

'Taliesin,' the land said, 'limned my forms.
My metric moves lyrical to slide a bard's tongue.
My maps are only sunlight: my only frame,
a poet's making. How else render an essence
within fact's borders? What customs posts,
what goods and traffic can congeal a dream?
My emblem is gaunt upland: my metaphor,
valleys of lost content. I exist ample
as the mind's abundant seasons: I lie fertile
as fruitfulness demands. I am
the unconquerable fief, a fiction's
unassailable kingdom. My only maps
are sunlight. All my roads and routes
become the labyrinths that lead always
inward into a minstrel's mysteries.'

Do you fancy a drink?

No loving cup this,
myth's blood-jug
for chivalry's silly search,
whose enigmatic cargo,
thorn and whimsy ferried
sparks ineffable
in a new weather's mists,
perching its aureole
untransubstantiated on
a void altar, its blood
a scrape of coloured ink
staining lost parchments,
its gold transmuted
to alchemic dream,
its jewels now material
as a conjuror's fire.

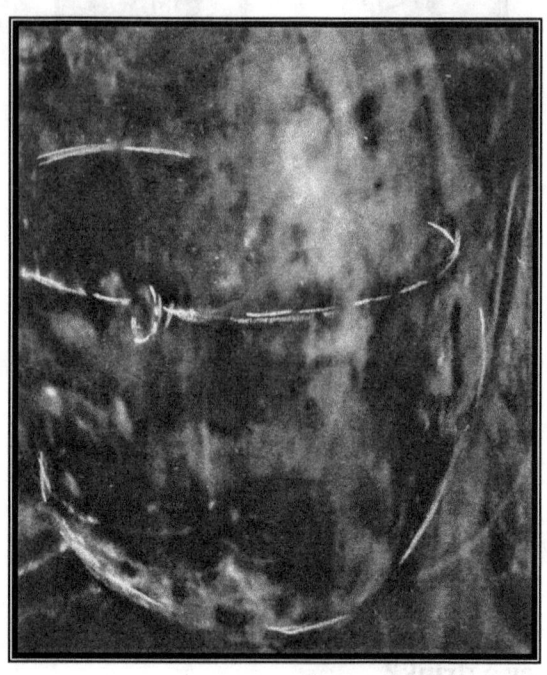

A cup's circumference

'My business,' she said, 'is circumference.
I am mythical and complex. Guess at
my mistranslations, divine the regiments
of fools and sages who have hunted my grace.
I am oblivion: I am salvation: I am cash.
My million acolytes are drawn magnetically
to an imagined lustre. Bran came: the Fisher King,
armies of knights and nuns, ascetics by the score:
dunces and freaks. *Did they learn anything?*
Most found what they intended to find. Many
discovered the need of their need. I had
no hand in that. *And did it ever matter?*
Some craved healing: some sought cures
to salve their impotence: some saw the Host:

some believed that never-ending sustenance
would benison their dream. And you, reader,
will pattern what you expected and create
the pattern that creates your expectation.'

Morgan le Fay: My Sonar Acrobatics

Find me. I am unfindable.
Know me. I am not knowable. I
am amorphous black. I am
translucent. My form's metaphor
outdances geometry. My mind's
figure disdains quantities.
The algebra that spells my hand
is anagram, the calculus
of my being the acrostic

of ever and never, of lie
and truth. I am various
and one, my face the black halo
unfilled. I dream the dream
in which you dream me, mirage adept
of else's bubble cauldron
that seethes or breeds the Grail. I am
plenty's ambiguous mother,
enigmatic abbess of dearth.
I am the old magic, consort
of Avalon's evanescence.
I am not knowable. Know me.
I am unfindable. Find me.

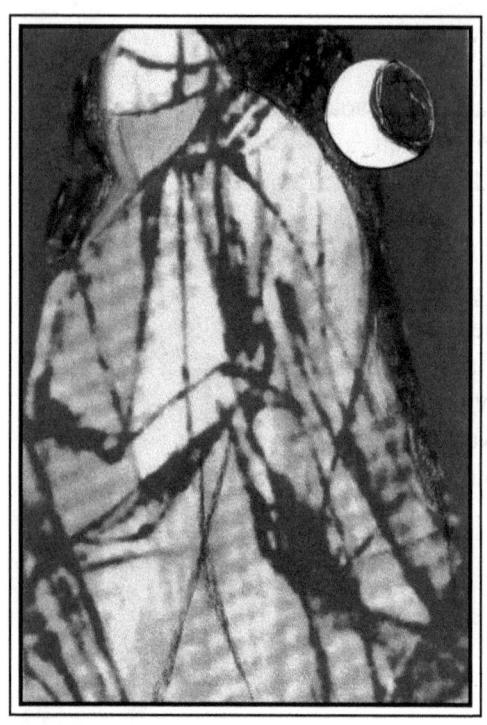

Morgana: the echo of an echo

'What metaphor of myself,' she said
'does my cloak conceal? I am complex
and multiple. My being is circumference.
I am the fluid adept of illusion,
inchoate in the shapes and states of else.
I am compass. Do you guess the trope
of my amorphousness, the rhetorics
of my unstable essence, the apologues
of my soul's labyrinths? I am chimera flesh.
I am the tongue's pentecosts. My sophistry
conjures annunciations. Find me:
I dance within an unreflecting mirror.
Hear me: I am the unreturning echo.'

Morgause: a Guide to Royal Incest

'It was,' she said, 'my sister's augury.
She dreamed a cauldron empty, old gods
irrelevant in a whirling world. A black sun
rowed in our sky, the great arteries
of our rivers writhed the strangulation
of a new magic's tourniquet. My sacrifice,
her cantrip told, though it must breed
the beast of incest, would spawn the cure
to medicine our kingdom's rot.
So my feigned ardour panting my brother
between my thighs. So in Camlan's wrestle,

the incest algebra of a mutual blood,
a diploid wounder and wounded
the father-uncle and the nephew-son.
contrive the contingent prophesy
inherent in her sanguine logarithm.
But still the sun's black asterisk rows
its long apostasy: still no apotheosis
leavens the land: still neither epiphany
nor enchantment levers to liquefy
our viscous arteries. *My sister lied.*'

A Handbook for Mycologists

Under a failing sun,
treachery's fungus spawns
in Camelot's soil. Lace
miasmas of bacterial taint
thread underground to swell
corruption's canker beneath
the roots and branches
of order's tree. Dishonour wrangles
anarchic in fetid air
and the tribes' resentments
fester in Arthur's garden.
It must come to this.
Betrayal's mildew bloats
in defeat. Excalibur's last thrust,

witched to a Judas-kiss,
is instrument of the wound
that catapult's waste's spores
into a protean air.

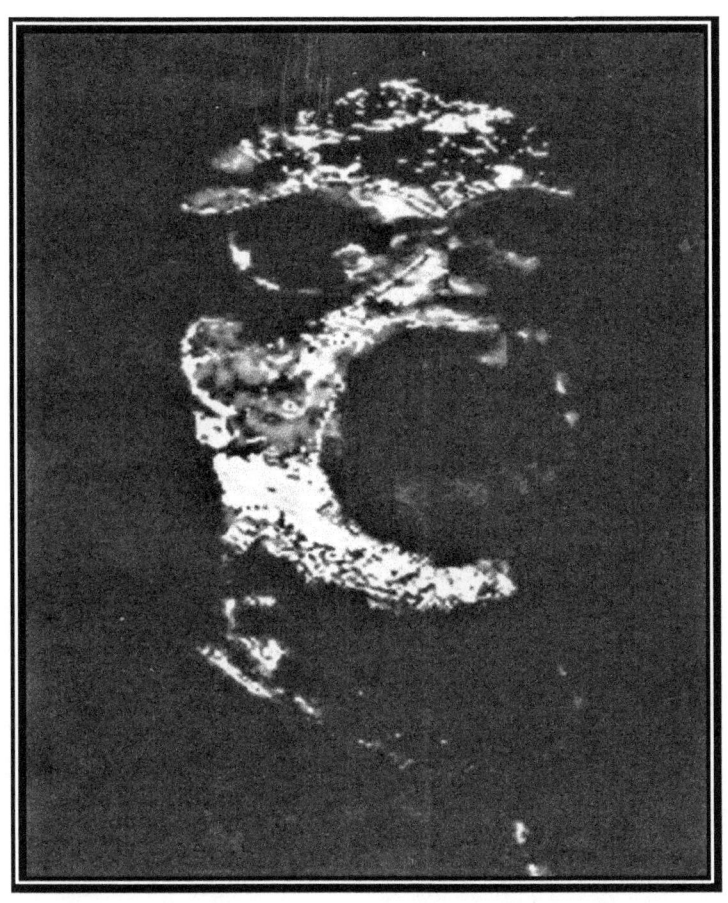

What you wear is what you are

'A king's skull,' he said, 'captains my mask. It is
my metaphor of power. Its features are
my features. It swears my right to fit it.
I am iron within iron. The snake head
is mine. It masks a venom. These adder scales
are my intentions' metaphor. My eyes,
unlidded, to shock back the sun, are blind
to pity or remorse. They stare my metaphor

of my resolve. My black mouth's tunnel
roars a locked scream of hate, its metal lips
assert a silent treachery, the stench bawl
of coming war and death. It is my metaphor
of my will. An old order is dying:
a round table rots to punk and chivalry
is a fop's game. The tribes are sick and need
a new healing. I am that healing.'

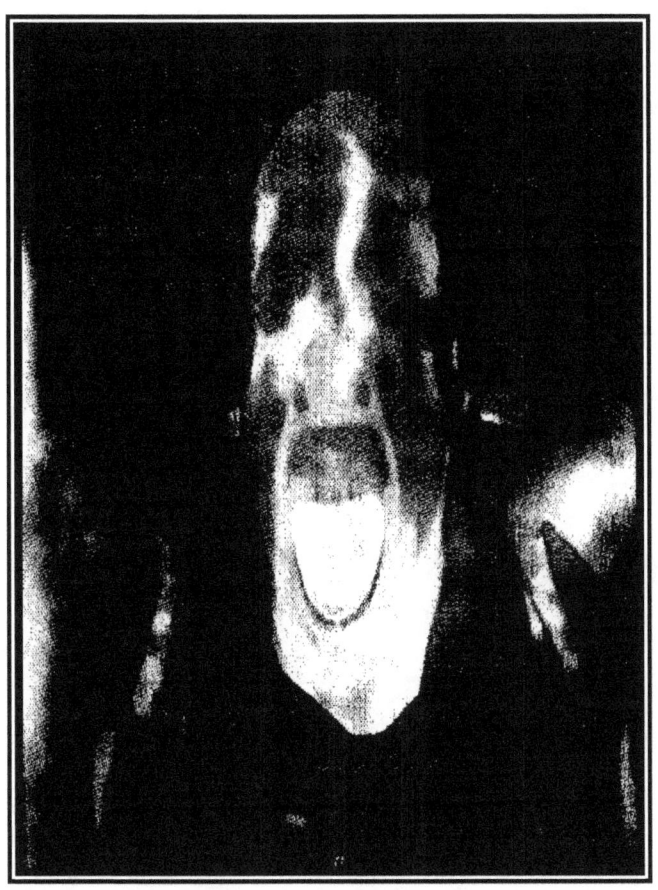

A Diploid Algebra

'I am,' the beast said, 'the Word. The Word
is incest. Incest spawns me, incest
my omen and amen. I am the incubus
of your lust, spat from and conceived by
your loins. Can you believe my being
burns in your thrust between your sister's thighs?
Can you guess my lewd conception
within her panting compliance? Chaos
surges my veins: my flesh is treachery:

dishonour propels my slime element.
Ploughing and seeding of a corrupted field
spews my infected crop. Already,
your kingdom rots: already, the twisted root
ferments a twisted seed. I hear
an adder's hiss: I smell your bastard's treason
for power: I foresee death and deceit.
There can be no renounce. I am the flesh
made Word: I am the Word made flesh.'

Mere Manipulation

Arthur's Kingship embalmed
in Avalon's cold storage,
she reclaims her doze,
shivering in the liquid drifts
of time's nectar capsule,
once more pulsing pendulum
to the fluid mechanisms
of a conjuror's clepsydra.

The sword lobbed and caught,
its enigma again wombed
in her jealous ownership,
she lies embryo, suspended
within the juice languor of
myth's amniotic caisson.
Her legend usefulness
now redundant, Merlin broken
and Lancelot shrunk to be
a whore's puppet, she sways
a bubble nothingness, slung in
the hydraulic hammock
of miasmic currents,
captive to the sorceries
and salts of fabulous tides.

Nimue sees Darwin right

'*Tadpole,*' she says, 'I watched you swim.
I am the world's water-myth, timeless Nimue.
The ripples you dream my face are sorceries.
I am fluid and multiple, my alchemy sunk
deeper than Lyonnesse.
                    Tadpole,' she says,
'I watched your clumsy grope to mud. Ask me
how many lives have bulged my sea. I remember
all my children. Faceless Viviane, I am
the green rainbow, submarine and cool.
My face you dream is a weed's trick. No ink
corrupts my annals.
                    Tadpole,' she says,
'I watched your lurch and hop to air.
 I am your mother's mother. You left me.'

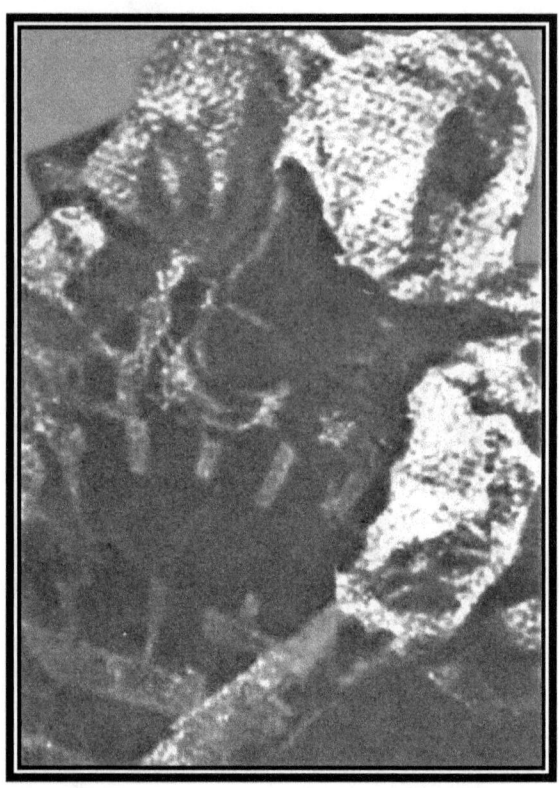

Making a Splash

'I almost believed,' he said, 'and I preferred
the old magic. Its gods wore human flaws.
We dreamed the everlasting cauldron to supply
our tribes with food, unbreakable swords,
Llew's imperial queen the divinities fashioned
from birds and flowers. They were rich lies
to roister my mabinogian days. But
it was a hard time for kingship. Truth was changing.
The old maps led nowhere: the past's cosmologies

were manifestly false: constellations
rattled a darker order. Then with their myths
of a new magic, the Frenchmen came.
They dreamed a grail and not a cauldron, a rood
to replace the sword, a virgin birth unlike
our queen of feathers. When a black sun
rowed in our sky, the earth trembled. Dishonour
marched rampant through us. It had to come
to Camlan's bloodfest. All the false gods
were hovering there. When he told me
to arch his sword to the mere, the branch I threw
slapped a sufficient splash. How could I know
which magic I was serving, what myths
or mysteries march covert in this world?'

An Allegorical Analogue

'You must take,' the island said, 'the barque
Impossible. Sail for terrain that reaches
inexorably to Heaven. Set your course
to truths that cannot exist. Know that I am
a fantasy. In me, the universe
packs intensified dimensions. How do you
conceive the stars, or hear a fugue or read
a metaphor? I am the bubble dream,
the never-never utopia that sustains
your undead, available only
to the oppressed, the disinherited.

Remember this: I am a mirage, an island
of the mind's invention. *Be aware of this:*
my ports allow no emigration.
Never forget: no drum wakens the dead.'

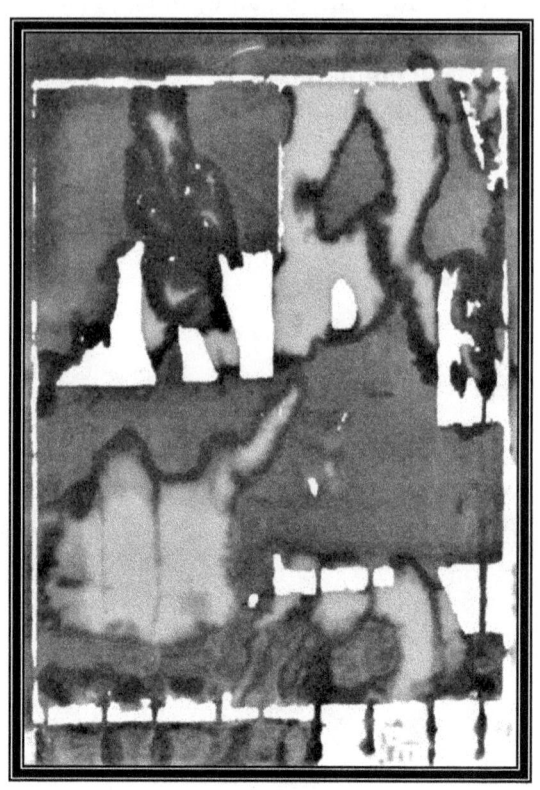

The Thigh in the Wound

'Your Royal Highness,' he said, 'I address
the state of the nation. Sadly, the cure
of your injury and ailment is unlikely
to be soon discovered. The Thatched dwellings
of villages and cities, rotten in their conception,
are ruinous and their architectures,
from the first corrupt, now stink in decay.
The poor, as we have always demanded,
are unaware of principle and properly, the rich

lack conviction. There have developed
rituals for those who live as cattle. In short
the falcon of order has fucked off. The thigh,
female and frequently open and usually
titillatingly displayed, is now the wound.
The counter-eugenic follies and policies
of our shrinking manufacture have borne
their inevitable and illegitimate fruits.
Corrupted estates stretch in a shit-stained
bandage to defile the fields and woodland
where supermarket trolleys parcel
and cage the water-table. Foreign agents
have been successful in their introduction
of an emin squalor into galleries and libraries.
Usury is rife, its philistines well-rewarded
and hygienically protected. Lust and envy
in their various fashions cosmetically control
much of what is projected or printed.
The gardens of greed and ignorance
are carefully nurtured, their deliberate soil
knowingly alloyed and daily manured.
Pornography and celebrity
in their twin cannibalisms swell
a jordan inflation. We now need to recognise
that the construction and worship
of false gods has become our most successful
and profitable fabrication industry.
The change that might have healed your wound
has either frozen or fused. Since then,
the world turned upside down. A new beast,
so we are told, slouches somewhere,
but we have lost both bestiary and map.'

76

www.ingramcontent.com/pod-product-compliance
Lightning Source LLC
Chambersburg PA
CBHW071410040426
42444CB00009B/2189